TURTLES

(A Fascinating Book Containing Turtle Facts, Trivia, Images & Memory Recall Quiz: Suitable for Adults & Children)

By

Matthew Harper

Image Courtesy of feraliminal

For legal reasons we are obliged to state the following:

Copyright 2014 Matthew Harper

ISBN-13: 978-1500228149

ISBN-10: 1500228141

All rights reserved. No reproduction, copying or transmission of this publication, CD's or DVD included in this system may be made without written permission. No paragraph of this publication may be reproduced, copied or transmitted without written permission, or in accordance with the Copyright Act 1956 (amended).

Hi and a very warm welcome to "Turtles".

I'm one of those people who loves to hear about extraordinary facts or trivia about anything. They seem to be one of the few things my memory can actually recall. I'm not sure if it's to do with the shock or the "WoW" factor but for some reason my brain seems to store at least some of it for a later date.

I've always been a great believer in that whatever the subject, if a good teacher can inspire you and hold your attention, then you'll learn! Now I'm not a teacher but the system I've used in previous publications on Amazon seems to work well, particularly with children.

This edition includes a selection of those "WoW" facts combined with some pretty awesome pictures, if I say so myself! At the end there is a short "True or False" quiz to check memory recall and to help cement some of the information included in the book. Don't worry though, it's a bit of fun but at the same time, it helps to check your understanding.

Please note that if you're an expert on this subject then you may not find anything new here. If however you enjoy hearing sensational and extraordinary trivia and you like looking at some great pictures then I think you'll love it.

Matt.

I thought that before we get down to some of those amazing turtle facts, we might begin with some snapshots of the different types, just to get the juices flowing……….

SPOTTED TURTLE

Image Courtesy of Derrick Coetzee

PAINTED TURTLE

Image Courtesy of U. S. Fish and Wildlife Service - Northeast Region

GREEN TURTLE

BOX TURTLE

ALLIGATOR SNAPPING TURTLE

LEATHERBACK SEA TURTLE

Image Courtesy of USFWS Headquarters

SLIDER TURTLE

Image Courtesy of LabyrinthX

LOGGERHEAD TURTLE

HAWKSBILL TURTLE

OLIVE RIDLEY TURTLE

Image Courtesy of jurvetson

Okay, that's it for the warm up, let's get on with the game......

Image Courtesy of Scout

Did you know that turtles are thought to date back 220 million years?

Image Courtesy of Brett Hammond

Did you know that a turtle's body temperature can vary depending on its surroundings?

Image Courtesy of MyFWCmedia

Did you know that turtles never lay their eggs in water?

Image Courtesy of Deepwater Horizon Response

Did you know that most land dwelling turtle's eyes are constantly looking down to see objects in front of them, while turtles who live mostly in water have eyes at the top of their head?

Image Courtesy of wolfpix

Did you know that turtles can retract their heads in one of two ways; backwards under the spine or to the side?

Image Courtesy of L'eau Bleue

Did you know the largest ever sea turtle measured fifteen feet long?

Image Courtesy of rogerimp

Did you know that the heaviest living sea turtle weighs over 900 kilograms?

Image Courtesy of jencu

Did you know that the top half of a turtle's shell is called the carapace?

Image Courtesy of pwmeek

Did you know that the inside of a turtle's shell contains around sixty bones?

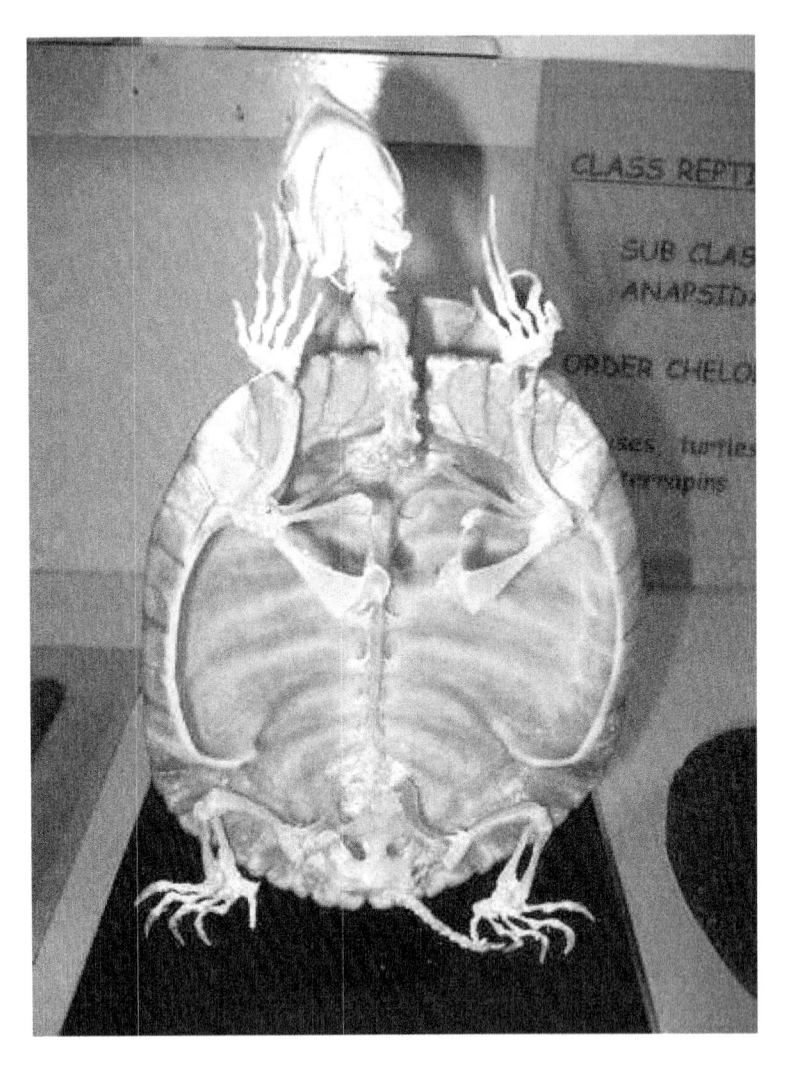

Image Courtesy of robstephaustralia

Did you know that young turtles are carnivorous?

Image Courtesy of Tobyotter

Did you know in the USA, it is illegal for anyone to sell a turtle under four inches long due to a 1975 law, but a loophole allows people to sell them in flea markets for educational purposes?

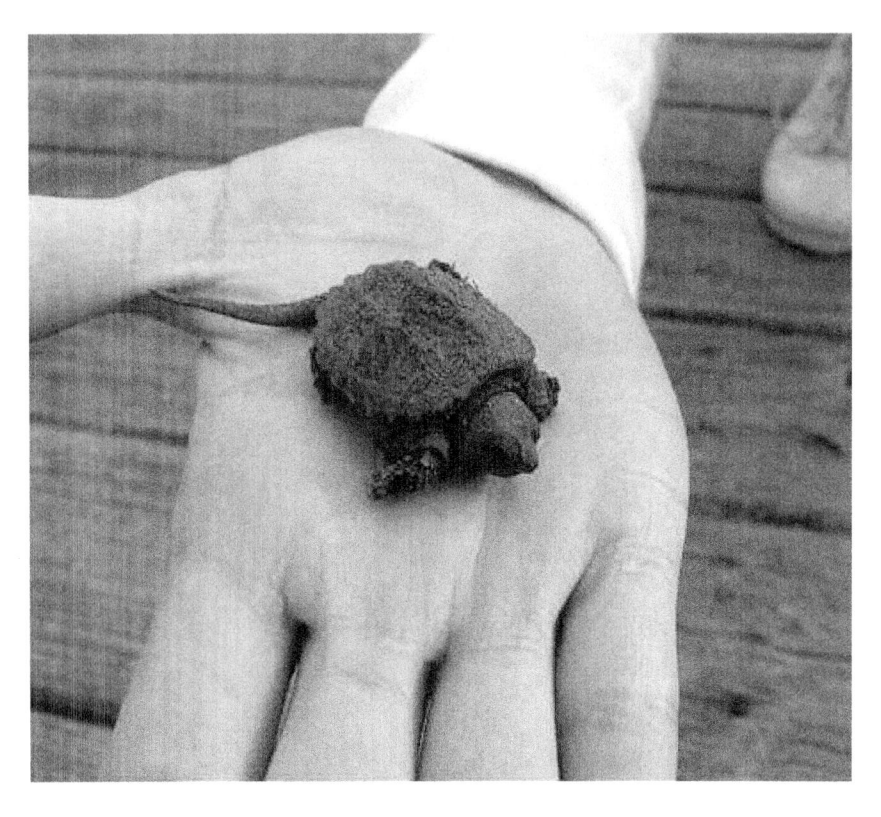

Image Courtesy of John Winkelman

Did you know that a turtle farm was built on the island of Grand Cayman purely for the purpose of rearing sea turtles for meat? YUK!

Image Courtesy of The Original Turtle

Did you know that in a report published in 2011, 48-56% of all species of turtle are thought to be endangered?

Image Courtesy of Sarunas Burdulis

Did you know that the first turtles on earth could not retract their heads? This only came about through evolution.

Image Courtesy of Earthrace Conservation

Did you know the only continent that turtles do not live on is Antarctica?

Image Courtesy of kayadams.com

Did you know the smallest turtle is called the Bog Turtle?

Did you know that the plates of a turtle's shell are called scutes?

Image Courtesy of Furryscaly

Did you know that most turtles have five toes on each foot but there are a small number that only have three?

Image Courtesy of edenpictures

Did you know that a turtle's shell contains nerve endings that help its senses?

Image Courtesy of steve lodefink

Did you know that the Alligator Snapping Turtle lures insects and small animals by wiggling its tongue? They then think it looks like a worm and move within reach of its sharp claws.

Image Courtesy of Norbert Nagel, Morfelden Walldorf, Germany

Did you know that turtles are endothermic (cold blooded)?

Image Courtesy of zdw

Did you know that marine and land turtles are classified as "Order Testudines", which is a class of animal that has a shell which forms part of the ribcage?

Image Courtesy of wollombi

Did you know although modern turtles do not have teeth, fossils of the earliest turtles have been found with teeth?

Image Courtesy of IvanWalsh.com

Did you know that there are only seven different species of sea turtle?

Image Courtesy of motleypixel

Did you know that turtles can be aged anywhere between five and thirty five before they are ready to breed?

Image Courtesy of Daryl Wallace

Did you know that female sea turtles go back to the beach they were born on to lay their eggs?

Image Courtesy of puuikibeach

Did you know that sea turtle eggs take between forty to seventy days to hatch?

Image Courtesy of EraPhernalia Vintage

Did you know that a turtle's gender is decided by the temperature of the sand it is incubated in?

Image Courtesy of Anosmia

Did you know that all but the Flatback Sea Turtle can be found in the USA ?

Image Courtesy of Purpleturtle57

Did you know that some turtles can swim at speeds of up to 35 miles per hour?

Image Courtesy of lakshmioct01

Did you know that turtles can dive up to 3000 feet below sea level?

Image Courtesy of NOAA's National Ocean Service

Did you know that according to Federal records, American aircrafts hit 4 turtles a year during take off or landing?

Image Courtesy of USDAgov

Did you know that when turtles return from migration they are able to return to exactly the same spot they left from?

Image Courtesy of puuikibeach

Did you know that the name for a group of turtles is a bale?

Image Courtesy of cygnus921

Did you know that out of every one thousand baby turtles only one or two live to be adults?

Did you know that 1990 saw a peak in the sale of turtles as pets due to the Teenage Mutant Ninja Turtles movie?

Image Courtesy of ianmalcm

Did you know that in Australia, you need to have a Reptile Licence to own a turtle?

Image Courtesy of JamieDrakePhotos

Did you know that when swimming underwater for long periods, up to nine minutes can pass between a turtle's heartbeats?

Image Courtesy of wwarby

Did you know the lower part of a turtle's shell is called plastron?

Image Courtesy of Scott Penner

Did you know that a three headed turtle was discovered in a pond in Taiwan in 1999?

Image Courtesy of woth1000.com

Did you know that despite not having vocal chords, the giant musk turtle is known to yip like a dog when under attack and the female leatherback sea turtle has been known to make a noise that resembles a human burp?

Giant Musk Turtle

Image Courtesy of L.A. Dawson

Did you know that turtles select their mates by smelling their tails?

Image Courtesy of Kevin Burkett

Did you know that even though they have no ears, turtles can hear sounds ranging from 50 to 1500hz?

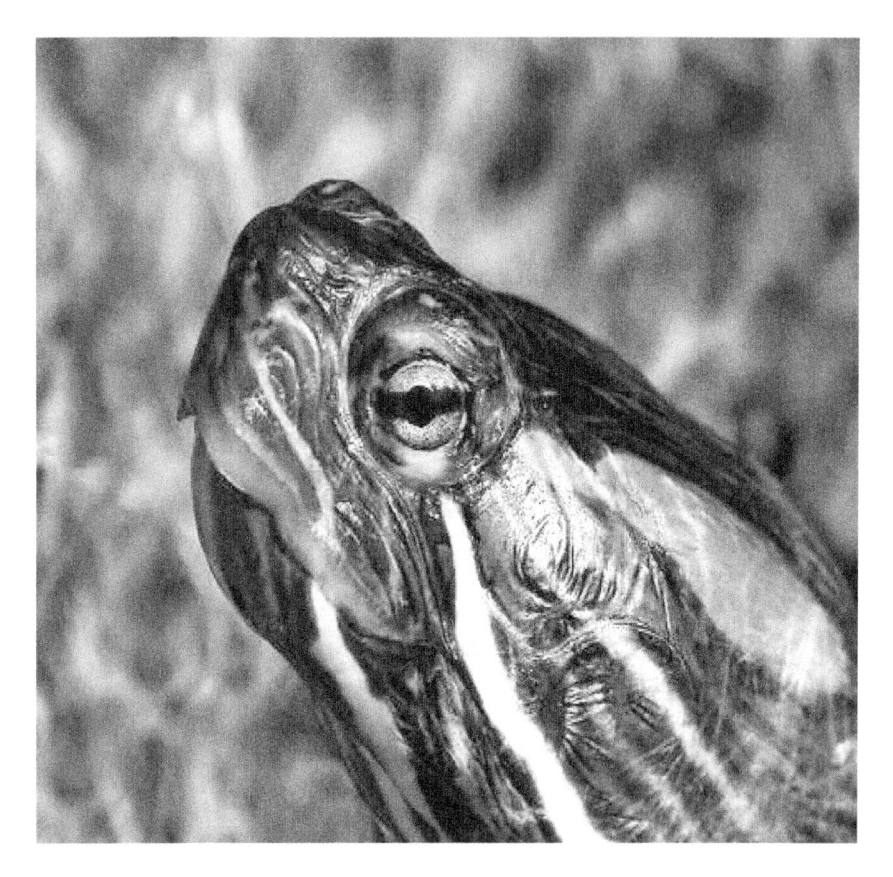

Image Courtesy of SidPix

Did you know that unlike most air breathing creatures, turtles don't have a diaphragm so must move their head and limbs to help them breathe?

Image Courtesy of notsogoodphotography

Did you know that turtles have favourite colours? Red, Orange and Yellow items have caused great interest from turtles during research?

Image Courtesy of cliff1066

Did you know that the African Helmeted Turtle has four glands under its legs that secrete a nasty smelling liquid that even horses have been found to be repulsed by?

Image Courtesy of Greg Hume

Did you know sea turtles have special glands to remove salt from the water they drink?

Image Courtesy of Wootang01

Did you know that the Western Painted Turtle can survive for around four months without oxygen if kept at 37 degrees Fahrenheit?

Did you know that of the 7 different species of marine turtle, 6 of them can be located on the Great Barrier Reef?

Image Courtesy of Ippei & Janine Naoi

Did you know that a marine turtle's diet consists mainly of sea grass and jellyfish?

Image Courtesy of wwarby

That's about it for the turtle trivia for now. I'd like to finish this publication with TEN "True or False" questions based on what you've just read. It should help you to really cement the information and to test your memory recall!

....
....

DON'T FORGET TO KEEP YOUR SCORE: THERE'S 1 POINT FOR EACH OF THE FIRST 9 QUESTIONS AND 5 POINTS FOR THE BONUS QUESTION GIVING A TOTAL OF 14 POINTS ....

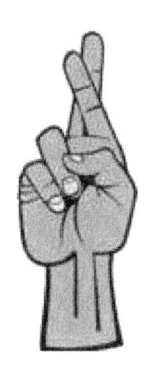

1.

TRUE or FALSE: Turtles are thought to date back 220 thousand years.

FALSE

Turtles are thought to date back 220 **MILLION** years.

2.

TRUE or FALSE: Turtles never lay their eggs in water.

TRUE

3.

TRUE or FALSE: The top half of a turtle's shell is called the car space.

FALSE

The top half of a turtle's shell is called the **CARAPACE**.

4.

TRUE or FALSE: The only continent that turtles do not live on is Africa.

FALSE

The only continent that turtles do not live on is **ANTARCTICA**.

5.

TRUE or FALSE: Female sea turtles go back to the beach they were born on to lay their eggs.

TRUE

6.

TRUE or FALSE: 1990 saw a peak in the sale of turtles as pets due to the Finding Nemo movie.

FALSE

1990 saw a peak in the sale of turtles as pets due to the **TEENAGE MUTANT NINJA TURTLE** movie.

7.

TRUE or FALSE: Turtles are totally deaf.

FALSE

Even though they have no ears, **turtles can hear sounds ranging from 50 to 1500hz.**

8.

TRUE or FALSE: Turtles have favourite colours? Red, Orange and Yellow items have caused great interest from turtles during research.

TRUE

9.

TRUE or FALSE: Sea Turtles have special glands to remove salt from the water they drink.

TRUE

10.

BONUS ROUND WORTH 5 POINTS

TRUE or FALSE: A GROUP OF TURTLES IS CALLED A BALE.

TRUE

Congratulations, you made it to the end!

I sincerely hope you enjoyed my little turtle project and that you learnt a thing or two. I certainly did when I was doing the research.

ADD UP YOUR SCORE NOW.

1 point for each of the first 9 correct answers plus 5 points for the bonus round giving a grand total of 14 points.

If you genuinely achieved 14 points then you are indeed a

"TURTLE MASTER".

8 to 13 points proves you are a **"TURTLE LEGEND"**.

4 to 7 points shows you are a **"TURTLE ENTHUSIAST"**.

0 to 3 points shows you are a **"TURTLE ADMIRER"**.

NICE WORK!

Matt.

Thank you once again for choosing this publication. If you enjoyed it then please let me know using the Customer Review Section through Amazon.

If you would like to read more of my work then simply type in my name using the Amazon Search Box and hopefully you'll find something else that "takes your fancy" or go directly to my website printed below.

Until we meet again,

Matthew Harper

www.matthewharper.info

Image Courtesy of feraliminal